MAGGIE the ANGEL PUP

This book is dedicated to all children whose furry friends have crossed over the rainbow Bridge. They'll always be with you in your memories and in spirit.

Title: Maggie the Angel Pup

Text and idea: Gil Evans
www.gilevans.net
gilholland@aol.com

Cover, layout, design, and illustrations: Hanna Kowalewska
hanna-kowalewska.com
kowalewska.books@gmail.com

First published 2023.

MAGGIE
the
ANGEL PUP

Maggie was a loving dog born on a farm in Ohio. As a pup, she was always getting into things. She loved to chew on everything!

She had a taste for sticks and rocks, but her favorite chew toy was her Dad's slippers. No matter where his slippers were, Maggie would find one and take it to her kennel to play with; chewing it and leaving it soaked.

Like humans, Maggie was like a child learning and growing up not knowing what she was put here to do with her life.

When her Dad would come home from work, he would go to put on his slippers, only finding one. He knew where the lost one was— all matted up in Maggie's kennel. He got mad and yelled,

"THAT DOG ATE MY SLIPPERS!"

Maggie was sad. She didn't understand why he was so angry. She only played with one, not both as she always left one for Dad.

Maggie's Dad tossed her outside and wouldn't let her in the house. She looked in the door window, sad and whining to come in, but no one was allowed to bring her in. Maggie was outside for days.

Maggie was so SAD, COLD, and LONELY.
She decided to wander off.

She walked for days through
woods and fields.

One day, a van pulled up.
Maggie was happy to see a human.

This human was different. They had something long and scary. The human chased Maggie and finally cornered her. They caught her with the scary pole, put her in a cage, and took Maggie to a place with lots of other dogs.

Maggie was SO SCARED.
The dogs would bark all day and night.
Maggie laid in the corner of her cage wishing she could just go home.

A few days later, Maggie's family saw her in the town's newspaper and drove to the dog pound to bring her home.

They snuck Maggie into the garage to hide her from their father.

It worked for a few days until Maggie got into the house.

Dad was at work and Maggie was happy to be home. She went back to being herself and grabbed Dad's new slipper.

She played with it all morning long. When the children got home from school, they saw Maggie sleeping with the slipper. They knew she would be in trouble, so they hid the slipper.

When the father got home, he got his slippers, but one was missing. He was so mad, he yelled to the children,

"WHERE IS MY SLIPPER?"

They looked at each other and said, “We don’t know.”

"WHERE IS THAT DOG?"

He stormed around the house and found the slipper all matted and chewed up.

He searched high and low for her and finally saw her hiding in the garage.

He called the dog pound, and they took Maggie away.

This time, the dog pound put Maggie on a very short list to either be adopted or it would be her end.

Maggie wished for someone to help her, and an angel came to Maggie and told her what her mission was.

TO HEAL SAD PEOPLE.

Maggie was excited but was in locked up this cage and unsure how she would get out. The angel assured her that someone in need would come for her.

The dog pound posted a photo in the town's newspaper of Maggie and a good family saw the post of Maggie.

THE TOWN TIMES

In the latest issue of the town's newspaper, Second Chance Shelter has shared some adorable dogs that are looking for loving families who can give them a forever home. "Visit our shelter, meet these pups in person, and let them change your life!"

They drove to see her.

The people came with a dog of their own. This dog was their picky dog, if she got along with Maggie, then they would bring her home.

Maggie slowly moved towards the dog,they sniffed each other and became instant friends.

The two dogs jumped in the truck, cuddled up next to each other, and fell fast asleep. The people brought Maggie home that day.

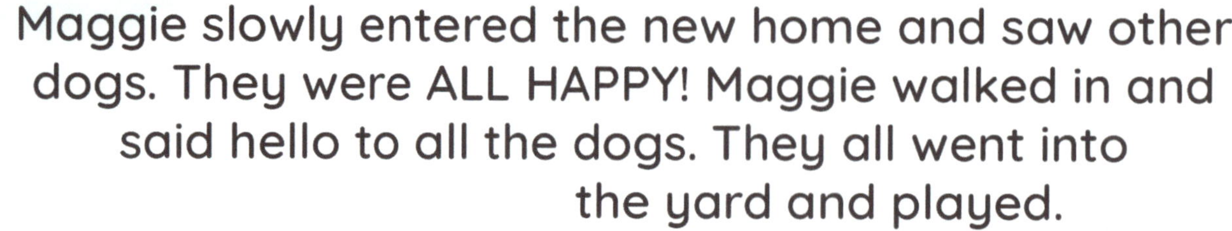

Maggie slowly entered the new home and saw other dogs. They were ALL HAPPY! Maggie walked in and said hello to all the dogs. They all went into the yard and played.

That day Maggie became part of the family. By now, Maggie was an older dog but found a home that loved her.

The humans LOVED MAGGIE SO MUCH, they let her lay with them on their couch, gave her baths, and let her sleep on their bed.

Maggie had SO MUCH LOVE for the humans and her new puppy sisters, she never had the urge to play with slippers.

Maggie moved into the home like an elderly nanny ready to take care of the children.

The family had their mother living in a small apartment connected to their home. She was old and frail. Maggie loved to go over and visit with the family's mother. Maggie loved it as the mother would have her morning tea, and toast. She always made sure she had an extra piece of buttered toast for Maggie.
Maggie would lay at her feet as the family visited her.

The human's mother was dying of old age, and Maggie was there to help them prepare for the mother's loss and the sadness afterward.
When she passed, Maggie knew it was her time to make sure the humans had the love and affection they needed to get through the pain. Maggie snuck up next to the daughter, and nuzzled her nose under her arm, to help ease her pain. She looked up at her with sad eyes letting her know she was there for her.

Maggie loved her humans so much; she spent all her time with them. She never left their side unless she was in the yard playing with her new sisters. Maggie brought so much happiness to the humans that she became the number one dog. Maggie realized she came to this family to help them with the sadness they had. She brought so much joy to them.

Maggie knew how to move into her human's space. She learned when they watch TV, that she could snuggle up next to them, lift their arm with her nose, and they would automatically start to scratch her not realizing what she did. Maggie melted her human's hearts, as she always laid in front of you with her tongue out and stared at you with her puppy eyes.

She knew when you were in pain and was always there to comfort you.

One day, Maggie got ill and was taken to the veterinarian's office to be checked out. Maggie was simply old, and when she came home, she continued to love the humans unconditionally. Maggie knew it would be soon that she would leave. She prepared her humans for her departure with her. She always followed their movement with her tired, sad eyes; quietly and peacefully laying down.

Maggie got weaker and weaker. She knew that she would not live much longer. She showed her humans that her time would soon end with them but assured them that she would return in their dreams and that she would be returning but starting a new life with another family, as their pet.

You see, Maggie was a healing dog, an angel, she was sent to be with humans to help them get through the hurt they had. She healed them with her unconditional LOVE and knew when it was time to go.

The humans she helped were sad, but they knew she was special, and she would return to become a new pup to help heal others.

Today Maggie lives with another family as a new pup. Maggie, like other pets, comes into our lives for a short time to help us get through tough times. Maggie leaves clues that she is still there, through the actions of their pets, sounds, and sometimes a quick view of her in the corner of your eye. There will be tiny feelings or behaviors that you will see.

BELIEVE IN YOUR THOUGHTS, IT'S THEM!

As our loving pets leave us, we need to remember that pets save and heal people from pain and sadness. Sometimes they stay for a long time and sadly, sometimes for a short amount of time. Maggie with us for four wonderful years.

We must remember this as we are lucky to be able to share the time with our pets knowing that each one is special and that they have a purpose to help so many.

Puppies can come into our life when we are babies to protect and love us through our youth. They are with us all the time and as we get older, we may move away from them learning new experiences in life. As we get older, they do too. It's this time that they prepare for their transition to leave our family. Our lives get busy, and we forget about them. When our pets get old and pass, we become sad and remember the good times we had with them as a child. These memories never leave us, they are there forever. Even in our busy world.

Every pet visits its humans through special memories and dreams. They never leave us; they always live in our hearts, and when we get old and it's our time to leave our bodies, Maggie and our other pets will be wagging their tails waiting for us...

Our Maggie will always be with us in our dreams and thoughts to help us mend our hurting, just like your best friend and Angel pup!

Aussie

Elli

Lucy, Sydney and Joe

Maggie

Mabel, Sydney and Elli

THE END

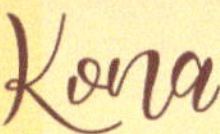

We invite you to add your angel pets photos to these frames.

www.ingramcontent.com/pod-product-compliance
Lightning Source LLC
Chambersburg PA
CBHW042050100726
47973CB00014B/207